Fashions of a Decade
The 1920s

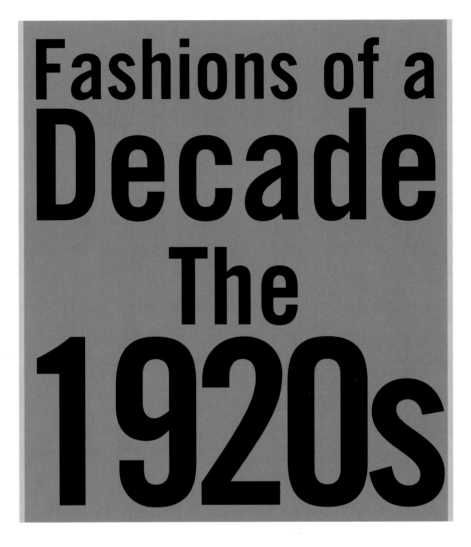

Fashions of a Decade
The 1920s

Jacqueline Herald

CHELSEA HOUSE
PUBLISHERS
An imprint of Infobase Publishing

Chelsea House
An imprint of Infobase Publishing
132 West 31st Street
New York NY 10001

Library of Congress Cataloging-in-Publication Data
Herald, Jacqueline.
    Fashions of a decade. The 1920s/Jacqueline Herald
    p. cm.
    Includes bibliographical references and index
    ISBN 0-8160-6718-X
    1. Clothing and dress—History—20th century—Juvenile
    literature. 2. Civilization, Modern—20th century—
    Juvenile literature. I. Title.
    GT596.H47   2006
    391.009/043—dc22   2006049932

Chelsea House books are available at special discounts when purchased in bulk quantities for businesses, associations, institutions, or sales promotions. Please call our Special Sales Department in New York at (212) 967-8800 or (800) 322-8755.

You can find Chelsea House on the World Wide Web at
http://www.chelseahouse.com

Author: Jacqueline Herald
Research for new edition: Kathy Elgin
Editor: Karen Taschek
Text design by Simon Borrough
Cover design by Dorothy M. Preston
Illustrations by Robert Price
Picture Research by Shelley Noronha

This new edition produced for Chelsea House by
Bailey Publishing Associates Ltd.

Printed in China through Morris Press, Ltd.

MP I SB 10 9 8 7 6 5 4 3 2 1

This book is printed on acid-free paper.

Contents

	Introduction	6
1	Flappers	28
2	The Perfect Gentleman	32
3	Stars of Stage and Screen	36
4	Chic Parisienne	40
5	Tutmania and All That Jazz	44
6	Skin Deep	48
7	In Search of Sun and Sport	50
8	Alternative Dressing	56
	Chronology	60
	Glossary	62
	Further Reading	63
	Acknowledgments	63
	Index	64

The 20s

This was the Jazz Age—the decade of the "flappers," as they were generally known, although Britain also knew them as "Bright Young Things." The 1920s opened with an explosion of color, the wailing sounds and fast rhythms of jazz, and the energetic dancing that went with it. This was a period of escapism, a youthful reaction against the dark and serious clothes, behavior, and mood of an older generation still clinging to old Victorian and Edwardian values. To the enthusiastic lyrics of "Everybody's Doing It Now," the new society hurtled through the twenties at an optimistic pace.

Suddenly the world seemed smaller. Internationalism—a move toward breaking down national boundaries in everything from finance to style—was a theme that ran through the decade. It was mostly an attitude of mind, but new practical links were made possible by developments in transportation. Auto racing became a popular and spectacular sport, while happy family motoring was enjoyed by many, thanks to Henry Ford's new, affordable Model T car. Passenger air travel began in the mid-twenties, though fashionable people with time on their hands still preferred to cruise at a more leisurely pace in expensively furnished private yachts and large ocean liners.

In European countries, which were still repaying the loans taken out to finance World War I and had little to invest in industry, industrial expansion was slow. In the United States, however, mass manufacture was well under way, using standardized, interchangeable parts, each of which was made using power-driven tools in a sequence of simplified mechanical operations. This "simplicity in multiplicity" was essential to achieve maximum efficiency and became known as the "American system." Henry Ford's Model T was so successful because it was a standard design, made of easily changeable parts.

▲ The fashionable crowd at this motor racing meeting in France, 1923, is wearing clothes influenced by those of the drivers. Along with leather jackets, coats, and scarves knotted casually around the neck, some people are even wearing helmets and goggles.

▲ The Model T Ford was available "in any color as long as it's black". Black was the only color of paint that would dry quickly enough to keep up with the production line seen here.

His success in catering to a mass market was due to his modern production system, in which operatives worked their apparatus at the pace of a moving assembly line, each worker adding one component in a systematic conveyor belt of production.

In terms of fashion and behavior, the 1920s appeared to be a decade of fun for the consumer, but beneath this jazzed-up facade were all kinds of social and moral tensions. In 1919, the Volstead Act had prohibited the sale but not the consumption of alcohol. Generally known as Prohibition, the ban lasted from 1920 to 1933. It had been introduced on moral grounds and to discourage the

▲ The transatlantic liners offered luxurious suites, first-class cuisine, sports facilities, and elegant ballrooms with their own dance bands.

Radio Concerts

When public broadcasting in Britain was launched in June 1920 by the nightingale voice of Australian prima donna Dame Nellie Melba singing "Addio" from *La Bohème*, radio stations were scattered irregularly around the nation and the number of households that could "tune in" was limited. In the United States, however, the opening of thousands of commercial radio stations meant that public broadcasts were much more regular and widespread. As more and more people began to enjoy broadcast music, their taste for jazz and new melodies became more diverse. On the negative side, instant rhythms at the turn of a knob—or the winding up of a 78 rpm gramophone—caused a decline in singing and piano playing at home and a steady reduction in the number of music and singing teachers. Few working-class homes, however, could yet afford a radio.

▲ The sale of sheet music for popular songs allowed enthusiastic dancers to provide their own accompaniment for practice at home.

8

growing criminality, which Congress blamed on the large consumption of alcohol throughout the country. However, the act had the opposite effect. As the sale of alcohol went underground, there was a huge increase in the illegal smuggling, manufacturing, and selling of what was known as "bootleg whiskey." Gangsters cashed in on this new business. Chicago's Al Capone was just one of the era's most notorious gangsters, his activities drawing the kind of media attention previously reserved for politicians and celebrities or for royalty.

The fact that so many Americans were drinking illegally during Prohibition, whether at home or in clubs called "speakeasies," bred a climate in which some aspects of criminal behavior became acceptable. This loosening of moral standards had a widespread impact on many people's approach to life, and perhaps to balance it, there was a growth of interest in fundamentalist Christian religions.

Showing One's Colors

Some aspects of pre-war fashion were rebelled against, while others, like driving hats and veils, took on a new inspirational role. Wartime garments also adopted a new look. Some men's clothes (knitted cardigans, for example) were re-invented as women's fashions. The practicality of the weatherproofed gabardine Burberry raincoat ensured that it would become an international classic of the future for men and women alike. Leather helmets, jackets, and coats worn for flying and driving became the trademarks of active sportswear. Iris Storm, the heroine of Michael Arlen's novel *The Green Hat* (based on the writer and campaigner for black causes Nancy Cunard), became a style icon in her leather jacket and green cloche hat. As the decade wore on, however, leather became associated with the military-style uniforms of the Nazi party, which was rising in popularity. The Nazis were one of several extremist right-wing German nationalist groups protesting against the collapse of the deutsch mark in 1923. The SA (storm troopers) wore over-the-knee leather "jackboots" with their brown uniforms and armbands displaying the party symbol, the swastika.

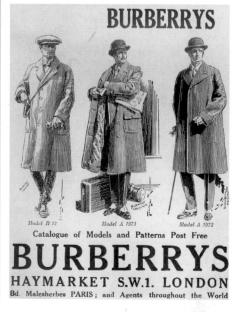

◄ As this smart Parisian lady is discovering, the appearance of the automobile brought its own hazards—crowded streets and traffic jams.

◄ Founded in 1856, the Burberry Company introduced its trademark red/camel/black-and-white check in the twenties as a lining for the trench coat.

► Classic day wear for ladies who lunch. Hats and a veil protect their complexions from the Riviera sun.

Meanwhile, in 1922, Benito Mussolini had become Italy's prime minister and Europe's first Fascist dictator. In what became known as the "top hat revolution," Mussolini marched into Rome with 22,000 black-shirted supporters who called him "Il Duce" (The Leader). Once in power, he continued to wear black but insisted on distinguishing himself by wearing a silk top hat. The Italians were the first to adopt Fascism, a system of nationalist and anti-Communist dictatorship. Fascism was most successful in countries like Italy and Germany, where high unemployment, extreme poverty, and low morale made people more easily convinced by the would-be dictators' promises to make their countries great again.

If black was the color of Fascism, green was the symbol of pacifism. White, on the other hand, was the color of the long robes and hoods with narrow eye slits worn by the members of America's Ku Klux Klan, a fanatical, racially and religiously intolerant organization originally founded in 1915 and revived in the twenties. Ironically, it was also the color of *khadi*, a humble, homespun cotton cloth worn by India's Mohandas K. (Mahatma) Gandhi as an anti-British gesture for which he was imprisoned in 1922. To Gandhi, tailored English clothes and cotton imported from the mills of Manchester represented the British political oppression from which his country was seeking independence. By contrast, Turkey's president Mustafa Kemal (Atatürk) looked on Western clothing as an essential part of his country's modernization program. He made wearing the fez—the men's hat that symbolized Islamic orthodoxy—a criminal offense and also discouraged women from wearing the face-covering veil of traditional Islam.

In the USSR, photographer Alexander Rodchenko developed a revolutionary kind of clothing for men, based on a coverall and worn with a flat cap. Rodchenko's fashion idea reflected the Communist ideology of power lying with the workers and the Soviet hope of an egalitarian future.

The Social Calendar

Though the phrase the "New Poor" was heard more and more frequently—in Europe at least—upper-class society still operated according to

▲ The Russian worker's cap became a fashion statement as well as a symbol of the revolution.

▼ Most families only used one tailor or dressmaker, who kept their measurements in his reference book.

Postwar Emancipation for Women

The devastating loss of so many men in World War I meant that in much of Europe, the female population outnumbered the male. The British fight for votes for women secured a major victory in 1918 when Parliament passed the Representation of the People Bill. However, it only applied to women over 30. The US Constitution's Nineteenth Amendment of 1920 enfranchised American women, and throughout the decade, a number of new laws helped to change women's status in society. The number of female undergraduates was still much lower than that of men, but women were beginning to enter male-dominated professions, although not without a battle. The exception was in the office, where male clerks were generally being replaced by women typists and secretaries. Although female doctors were still rare, birth control pioneers Margaret Sanger and Dr. Marie Stopes founded their first clinics in New York and London respectively.

▲ For hunting and shooting parties, tweed was durable and kept out the worst of the weather.

▲ A society wedding was the highlight of the season. Bridal wear varied greatly, but a calf-length satin dress was the popular choice, with a head-hugging veil.

◄ Office girls needed a whole new wardrobe of smart day wear—and the confidence to deal with new-fangled machines.

the pre-war social calendar. This pattern of events was what the top end of the fashion industry was built on. Spring-summer collections of model clothes were launched by the fashion houses in time for the new "season." This included grand balls, visits to the races—Saratoga, for example, or Ascot in England and Longchamps in France—garden parties and attendance at private views of art exhibitions. By July, society had moved to the country or to the new resorts on the French Riviera or Palm Beach, Florida. Autumn was devoted to hunting and shooting—perhaps in Scotland—before the well-connected returned to London, New York, Paris, and Rome for the winter.

Social convention demanded that clothes be appropriate for the time of day, the activity, or the formality of the occasion. Even housemaids were required to follow suit and had different uniforms for morning and afternoon. Generally, the higher someone's social rank, the more clothes they needed to meet society's demands and to impress.

The passport to social success was wealth—or marriage into the nobility. This is what Hollywood's Gloria Swanson did. Having secured her marriage to the Marquis de la Falaise de Coudray, a "docile nobleman with a reckless taste in spats," she was attended in her grand mansion by servants who wore eighteenth-century-style powdered wigs and satin knee breeches. Similarly, the French fashion designer Gabrielle (Coco) Chanel might never have made her mark without the financial backing of a rich lover. Perhaps because of her poor and

Paris Exhibition

The term Art Deco was coined from the *Exposition des Arts Décoratifs et Industriels Modernes* ("Exhibition of Modern Decorative and Industrial Arts"), held in Paris in 1925. A series of pavilions displayed an international selection of design talent and industry. Above all, France's lead in the field of haute couture was celebrated in two sections devoted to fashion: Le Grand Palais and Le Pavillon d'Elégance. The latter was decorated by couturiere Jeanne Lanvin and showed the work of more than 60 couturiers. The jury's report on fashion in the exhibition was "functionalism by day, fantasy by night." Amid sumptuous lacquer screens by Jean Dunand and the stylish bronze furniture of sculptor Armand Rateau, high-fashion clothes were displayed on ultra-modern forms designed by the sculptor Vigneau-Siégal. They were colored olive green, purple, gold, silver, or black, or left as natural wood.

▲Making an entrance at a fashionable party. For more discreet moments, the feather fan could offer privacy for a secret conversation or hide the face, leaving the eyes alone to send a message.

◀"Coco" Chanel, perhaps the most influential designer of her generation, steps out in her own smart but casual jersey clothing.

▶Fashion found its perfect backdrop in the Art Deco interiors of the sumptuous Paris Exhibition of 1925.

▲Two models from the fashion House of Beer take a walk in Montmartre, Paris. Collars are definitely the talking point in this collection.

unconventional background, though, Chanel was not afraid to shatter the formality of Paris's fashion establishment by introducing the "Apache" sweater—a casual sweater strikingly patterned with Native American-style motifs. Paul Poiret, Chanel's equally successful rival, accused her of making duchesses look like shopgirls and joked that her fashions represented a *pauvreté de luxe* ("luxurious poverty"—in other words, poverty for the rich!)

The Haute Couture Business

Immediately after World War I, there was a shortage of the materials and skills necessary to revitalize France's haute couture industry, the most expensive sector of the fashion industry. In the 1920s, since so many jobs in France depended on haute couture and the French reputation for fashion was so high, the French government encouraged banks to grant extended loans to the fashion trade. In order to monitor the working conditions of staff and to maintain high standards of workmanship, a professional association of Paris-based couturiers, the Chambre Syndicale de la Haute Couture Française, was established. As the market became more secure, the fashion industry grew rapidly until by 1927 it boasted 250,000 employees in Paris, distributed between the city's 2,000 workrooms, salons, and shops. But the Wall Street Crash of 1929 was a catastrophe for fashion, when suddenly 10,000 Parisians in the trade were unemployed.

By the 1920s, the structure of a haute couture fashion house fell into the following general pattern. One or two main salons were devoted to showing the season's collections of "model" garments. These were the prototypes, which were modeled by live models, known as "mannequins," who paraded through the salon in front of the clients. The choice of mannequin was vital to secure a sale; in the mid-twenties, Jean Patou employed some 32 mannequins—six of whom had tall "American" figures—to model the 450 dresses making up each collection. Haute couture was so expensive and exclusive because the clothes were based directly on these "model" garments and made specially to order. The client would choose a design and then be fitted for a copy of the model garment, which would then be made up in the fabric and color of her choice. Members of royalty were permitted exclusivity on their selections: their chosen design would be withdrawn so that nobody else could order a copy.

▲Orientally inspired evening gowns in rich lacquer red, by the House of Worth, 1923. The lavishly embroidered panels of diamanté and colored silks were crafted by specialty workshops that served the exclusive fashion houses of Paris and had existed since medieval times.

Clients were attended to personally, always by the same *vendeuse* (saleswoman) and a fitter, both of whom would develop an intimate knowledge of the client's taste, figure, and so forth. The vendeuse coordinated the whole order, from the choice of model gown or outfit, through three or more fittings, to the final delivery. She was assisted by a *seconde vendeuse*, who saw that all the details were completed according to the client's wishes. The fitter gave instructions to the *première main qualifiée*, the more senior of two qualified seamstresses, who were assisted by an *arpette*, an apprentice whose lowly job was to pick up the pins. The house also had a buyer, responsible for the purchase of all materials, from bolts of luxurious fabrics to notions such as beads, sequins, and feathers.

Fashion houses offered a very personal service to those who had the money and the time to attend so many fittings. Obviously, only a minority had access to these clothes, but through features in magazines, the great fashion houses influenced what everybody else aspired to. And although designs could be protected by copyright, it was difficult to stop the "pirating" of diluted or minimally changed designs by large-scale clothing manufacturers. The pirating of styles led to a flourishing industry in America, with manufacturers producing what are known as "knockoffs" in the "rag trade." Of course, the quality of cloth was difficult to mimic—especially the limited-edition fabrics designed by Rodier of France, handwoven exclusively for him by peasant women in Picardy. In the case of French designer Madeleine Vionnet, the cut and seaming of her garments was impossible for anyone else to understand, so her clothes were difficult to copy exactly.

Because these fashions demanded special accessories, shoes and handbags of matching colors would be ordered for each outfit. The accessory trade employed teams of fine craftspeople. Paris-based Ugo lo Monaco included hand-painted feathers and silk flowers in his embroidery, while Carlo Piatti of Como, Italy, was renowned for the embroidered silk shawls that were a speciality of his hometown.

Cutting Corners

Mass production was made possible both by the modernization of factories, mainly through electrification, and by the economical, tubular cut of women's wear. Simplicity of shape meant efficiency—a saving of time and energy. The loose fit meant that dresses could be manufactured in a standard range of sizes, requiring minimal adjustment to the individual figure. Although mass production made the latest fashion accessible to a wider buying public, there was still a big difference between haute couture and home dressmaking. To bridge the gap, some Parisian couturiers—among them Jean Patou—began to sell original models wholesale.

▼Corset fitters came into their own in the twenties. The flat-chested, hipless, boyish look was achieved only with much effort and some serious underpinning.

What joy to be fitted for corsets at home!

—at no extra cost

WHAT woman who has known the satisfaction of having a custom corset planned and adjusted in the privacy of her own home, will ever buy a corset any other way? Especially as it costs no more.

There is a NuBone Corsetiere near you who will call at your home at your convenience. She will study your requirements and from the measurements she takes, an expert designer will build a corset *especially for you*, which will give you a *more graceful figure* and *greater comfort* than you have ever had before.

That delightful combination of perfect freedom with adequate support which you find in a NuBone Corset, is made possible by the patented woven wire stay which can be had *only* in NuBone Corsets. This stay is very light and very strong, yet flexible as rubber, *in every direction*. In a NuBone there is absolutely no feeling of restraint—it is almost as if you had no corset on.

A written guarantee that NuBone Stays will not rust or break accompanies every NuBone Corset. This rustless feature permits frequent washing of a NuBone and prolongs its life.

Write for free booklets
"The Secret of Slenderness"
and "Style Book"

An Excellent Profession
Write to us for booklet, "Correct and a Profession". We may have an opening for a Corsetiere in your town.

NuBone
CORSETS
Not Sold in Stores
The NuBone Corset Company · Erie, Pa.

New York City : Aeolian Building, 33 West 42nd Street
Western Office and Plant, 3520 S. Main St., Los Angeles, Cal.
Canadian Office and Plant, St. Catharines, Ontario
Australia: L. L. Lucas & Co., Melbourne

A typical store might offer three types of service, in addition to ready-made garments. The most exclusive service was that of the Model Gown Salon, catering to traditional custom-made ("bespoke") dressmaking. Next, an inexpensive dressmaking department allowed the customer to choose a paper pattern and a length of cloth from the nearby fabric department to be made up in the store's workroom, the overall cost including one fitting. A third department offered a cut-and-fit service, where the customer could buy the pattern and necessary materials, and the store's workroom would cut, baste (sew loosely), and fit the garment, to be finished by the customer at home.

Paper patterns, like those of today, were modified versions of the *toiles* (pattern pieces cut out of calico) devised by the houses of established couturiers, and, like the new clothing factories, they made fashion accessible.

Despite mass production, the expansion of retail services, and the growing numbers of women sewing at home, professional dressmakers were still in demand, especially for wedding dresses. Although many of them set up shops or workrooms, others operated on the same basis as Victorian sewing ladies, visiting the house to make up or alter garments as required.

The New Consumer

The new consumerism did not just mean a revolution in product, but in how those products were marketed, and in this America led the way. Promotional articles appeared in women's magazines of the 1920s under titles like "Best Dressed Products Sell Best."

As we have seen, mass production meant more uniformity of design and standard sizing. An efficient system of garment construction was clearly argued in the manifestos written by Soviet fashion designers following the revolution of 1917 and subsequent civil war in the Soviet Union, where political rather than financial motivation spurred the clothing factories into action.

▲Mail order was a fast-growing business. *The National Style Book*, published in New York in 1924, made it possible for women all over the United States to have dresses like these sent to them in a matter of days.

► The graphic style of this poster by August Trueb, dating from January 1928 and advertising a Haid and Neu sewing machine, embodies the spirit of the machine age.

Sewing Goes Electric

In the 1920s, electricity revolutionized housework and factory production alike. For example, a new generation of sewing machines, each powered entirely by a small electric motor, went into production. The implications for home dressmakers, as well as machinists in clothing factories, were enormous. In the 1920s, middle-class women were the main target of the electrical household revolution; the first features to be electrified were lighting and water heating, and then came the first of those consumer goods that most home owners take for granted today. In 1921, the Women's Engineering Society in Britain held a competition for the invention and improvement of laborsaving devices for the home. Two years later, the American company Frigidaire brought out an electric icebox, the forerunner of the refrigerator.

Consumerism—at least according to manufacturers and retailers—was the key to emancipation and democracy. The sales war in cigarettes exploited the female market, with women coerced into smoking "to prevent sore throats" or as an aid to losing weight. Many brands offered collectable picture cards for children tucked inside each package, putting pressure on mothers to buy more packages to make up the set.

Window shopping became a new pastime. The introduction of plate glass made the small-paned windows and colonnades previously used in department stores look very old-fashioned. Window displays now featured clothes worn by life-size, flesh-colored dummies, painted with realistic hair and makeup. Occasionally, though, something more novel might be found. In Paris, fashion accessories were sometimes displayed on dolls with painted, cloth-covered faces, one of these being based on the famous cabaret singer Mistinguette.

17

Once enticed into the store, the modern shopper's life was easy. The new, rational sizing system even sorted customers into more clearly defined "types," according either to income bracket or, in the case of Bullock's Department Store in Los Angeles, six personality types. Those were: the Romantic, the Statuesque, the Artistic, the Picturesque, the Modern, and the Conventional. The Modern type was: "the fashionable type. The woman who can fit herself into the latest mold without discomfort. Just now shingle-bobbed. Boyish. Sleek. Skirts short when they are so. And longer than anybody's when they are so." On the other hand, the Artistic type was: "a bit enigmatic. Usually with a suggestion of the foreign. Usually dark-haired, dark-eyed. A type that may accept vivid colors, bizarre embroideries, eccentric jewelry. The artistic type welcomes the revivals of Egyptian, Russian, and Chinese motifs and colorings. Peasant necklines. Berets. Hand-loomed fabrics."

The new consumer responded positively to modern technology, including new forms of communication. Fashion magazines continued to provide an important source of ideas and information, and in the twenties these grew in number and variety. Articles focused on aspects of modern life, like the new

▲The ice-cream and soda counters of Liggett's drugstore, at the corner of 42nd Street and Madison Avenue, New York, are typical of the new, light, sparkling interiors that tempted consumers inside to spend.

◀ This silk-and-lamé evening coat, designed by Raoul Dufy in 1927, has a Japanese look. The straight-cut coat gives a slender silhouette, and the wide, kimono-like sleeves accentuate slim hips, as well as making it easy to slip on over an evening dress.

▲No fashionable woman, whether in the United States or Europe, would dream of buying a new dress without first consulting *Vogue* magazine.

sports and the clothes that went with them. And then toward the end of the decade, the crucial link between Hollywood and the fashion industry developed, with certain styles being christened with the names of the movie stars who wore them.

▲ "Le Black Bottom," the toast of Paris dance halls. Like the Charleston, the dance was introduced into Europe by professional African American entertainers from the United States and was considered rather scandalous by the older generation. Young people, however, danced till they dropped.

The Age of the Machine

Postwar modernism was based on admiration of the machine and the belief that new materials, mass production, and a degree of automation could improve the quality of life. This idea was expressed in twenties' transportation, architecture, and fashion alike. For instance, the work of American car manufacturer Henry Ford, Swiss architect Le Corbusier (Charles-Edouard Jeanneret), and French designer Coco Chanel were all, in their different ways, radical for their avoidance of excessive detail. Ford's functionalism was motivated by a desire to reach the mass market, while designers like Le Corbusier and Chanel saw a kind of beauty in the clean, simple line and efficiency of the machine, which could be reproduced in their work through the pure function of carefully chosen materials.

This "machine aesthetic," as it is known, was expressed throughout the visual arts. The jerky movements of dances like the Black Bottom, the craze for jumping on pogo sticks, the angular, stylized acting in silent movies, and the wearing of dresses with a metallic finish all seemed to echo the machine. In 1924, *Vogue* featured Chanel's steel beads and scarves as stiff as propellers tied into "airplane bows."

Sport for All

The twenties' innovations in sport and exercise make an impressive list: calisthenics (a form of gymnastic exercise), squash, mechanical horses, rowing machines, massage by wide electric belt, and last but not least, an enormous beach ball known as the "medicine ball." The youthful, healthy-minded search for sun and sport among the rich was heralded by the optimistic symbol of the rising sunburst—later to become a popular motif of Art Deco style. The new building program and the spread of suburbs meant that municipal golf courses, swimming pools, football stadiums, and other sports facilities were opening up, making leisure activities available to greater numbers of people. In both 1924 and 1928, "the greatest swimmer ever" came home from the Olympic Games with a handful of gold medals and world-beating records. His name was Johnny Weissmuller—though he was to become better known for his film role as Tarzan.

◄ Just the thing to be seen in at Palm Beach—a smart but casual three-piece suit along the lines of Coco Chanel's knitted jersey fashions, designed by the House of Worth. Suits like this were the favorite of older women, whose desire to shock had given way to a choice of elegance.

►The more athletic members of the social set were to be seen on the ski slopes in worsted outfits that look more suitable for horseback riding—a far cry from today's figure-hugging suits.

Time and motion studies were applied not just to machines in the modern factory, but to the human form. In an article called "The New Body" in the avant-garde journal *L'Esprit Nouveau* in 1922, Dr. Pierre Winter, a doctor friend of Le Corbusier, announced: "Sport brings an element of order into life…. It demands the demolition of outworn framework. It introduces the law of balance which governs work and repose. It imparts precision and coordination to our movements. It trains us in quick reactions. It gives the time factor its fitting place in modern life."

The machine was also the key to mass manufacture, to the democratization of fashion. The Soviet Constructivist artist Varvara Stepanova, who was involved in designing textiles and clothing in the post-revolutionary spirit of the 1920s, stated in 1919: "Today's dress must be seen in action—beyond

this there is no dress, just as the machine cannot be conceived outside the work it is supposed to be doing…. Aesthetic aspects must be replaced by the actual process of sewing. Let me explain: don't stick ornaments onto the dress; the seams themselves—which are essential to the cut—give the dress form. Expose the ways in which the dress is sewn, its fasteners, etc., just as such things are clearly visible in a machine."

And so in the 1920s, fashion blended with the world of industrial design. The division of labor was considered a necessary part of production in this new machine age. Although his shoes were still being made by hand, Italy's Salvatore Ferragamo decided to change the organization of his workshop to improve efficiency. Whereas the cutting of the vamp (the front part of the shoe's upper), the piecing together, and stitching of the various parts had previously all been done by one person, Ferragamo decided to assign the individual tasks to separate craftspeople. In Paris, Madeleine Vionnet built an American factory behind her private mansion in the Avenue Montaigne. Her workforce of about 1,000 employees was treated to the healthiest facilities: a dispensary and dental clinic were attached to the workrooms, where a ventilation system changed the air at three-minute intervals to rid it of any infectious germs harbored in the fabric.

Fashion and the Arts

The Jazz Age spread from the United States to Europe in 1919, when the all-white Original Dixieland Jazz Band, which had created a sensation in Chicago and New York three years previously, opened a three-month season at the Hammersmith Palais de Danse in London. Playing by ear—since not one musician in the band could read music—their spine-tingling notes on trumpets and saxophones attracted a full house every night. But in most people's minds, jazz was associated with the revival of African American music in New York's Harlem.

The stage show the "Revue Nègre" came to Paris in the 1920s, just as jazz was taking off. Its star, the African American Josephine Baker, sparkled in fashionable white society

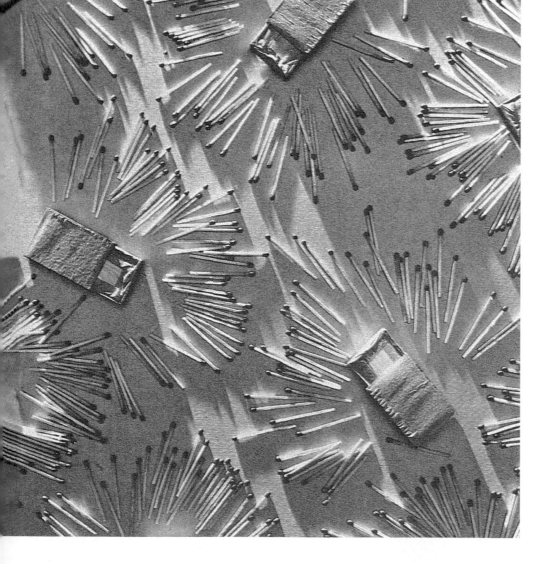

▼This extraordinary American trompe l'oeil design, "Matches and Match Boxes," was taken from a photograph by Edward Steichen and printed on dress silk. It was made by the Stehli Silk Corporation around 1928.

while entertaining with her own jazzy interpretation of the vogue for "African" culture. Wearing outrageous costumes, exotic tropical plumage—and sometimes very little at all—she was described as "a woman possessed … a shining *machine à danser* … all joint and no bones." She was at one moment the fashion artist's model, the next Picasso's.

This general enthusiasm for black and other non-European cultures was reflected in the new exhibitions in Paris. The Musée de l'Homme (Museum of Mankind) and smaller galleries displayed the art of Africa for the benefit of avant-garde artists and collectors alike. In 1922, an exhibition of African art from the French colonies featured tribal masks and sculpture. Three years later, the Galéric Ritlinger's exhibition of Indonesian art from the islands of Java and Bali started a fashion for batik (where a design is drawn in wax before fabric is dyed).

Paris was the international center of culture and experimental art. Artists and writers of all nationalities came to soak up the avant-garde atmosphere, and many settled there. Fashion designers were quick to name their latest printed fabrics after the newest art movements like "Futurist," "Cubist," or "Surreal."

There was a fruitful mixing of ideas from different art forms. For example, Russian ballet impresario Serge Diaghilev produced a ballet called *Le Train Bleu* in 1924, which had a front curtain designed by Pablo Picasso and costumes by Coco

▲French illustrator Thayaht matches the intricate cut and machine-like precision of this tailored autumn outfit by Madeleine Vionnet with his own mechanical style.

◀ British ceramics designer Clarice Cliff summed up the carefree enthusiasm of the age in her "Age of Jazz" figures. Now very rare, the complete set comprises dancers and orchestra members.

▲Erté's work blurred the lines between fashion illustration and the even more exotic worlds of ballet and the Folies Bergères.

St. Valentine's Day Massacre

As Prohibition sent the sale of alcohol underground, intense rivalry sprang up among the gangs of the major cities, who strove ruthlessly to get control of illegal liquor traffic. On February 14, 1929—Valentine's Day—in Chicago, seven unarmed bootleggers from the "Bugs" Moran gang were lined up against a garage wall and shot by members of Al Capone's gang, disguised as policemen. The most brutal and cold-blooded of the many highly publicized gangland killings, the St. Valentine's Day Massacre came to typify the violence of the Prohibition era in Chicago.

Chanel, based on her jersey sportswear. The vibrant colors and designs of Diaghilev's earlier productions, which had created a sensation before the war, continued to be reflected in the decorative arts throughout the twenties. Not only did fashion artists take inspiration from painters—Italian-born Elsa Schiaparelli from Spain's Surrealist Salvador Dalí, for instance— but the great couturiers, notably Jacques Doucet, were among the leading art patrons of the day.

In fashion illustration, artist Erté (Romain de Tirtoff) created fantastic effects in stage and costume design for France's Folies Bergères and later for America's Ziegfeld Follies. He also illustrated covers for *Harper's Bazaar*, while the cover of *Vogue* bore the art of Georges Lepape, Benito, and occasionally non-fashion artists like Giorgio de Chirico. During the first half of the decade, drawing was the main channel for fashion ideas, and some of the most colorful and stylish illustrations were produced by the *pochoir* process (a method of stenciling). Some of the finest examples can be found in the exclusive French journals *La Gazette du Bon Ton* and *Art Goût Beauté*.

Fashion photography was a new challenge, used initially to surreal effect by avant-garde photographers rather than as an accurate record of the latest designs. As the decade progressed, however, more photographers became interested in fashion, including Edward Steichen, Man Ray, Baron de Meyer, George Hoyningen-Huene, and Cecil Beaton. Steichen and De Meyer were enormously influential in the early years, succeeding each other as chief photographer for American publisher Condé Nast (De Meyer left for Hollywood and was then employed by *Harper's Bazaar*). London-based Beaton created theatrical effects, often devising painted or paper cutout backdrops for his portraits of society women. In 1925, Hoyningen-Huene joined *Vogue* in Paris but broke away from the confines of the studio to capture aspects of metropolitan lifestyle or a bird's-eye view of bathers on a beach. Experimenting with lighting and playing with differences of scale, Man Ray evoked the surreal quality of fashion itself. In 1929, he was joined by fellow American Lee Miller—the first woman to make an impact in the world of fashion photography.

Nightclubs

By the late twenties, Josephine Baker's success led her to open her own nightclub in Paris. She would arrive in her chauffeur-driven Voisin car, its brown

The First "Talkie"

"Wait a minute. You ain't heard nothin' yet!" were the first words spoken on-screen by Al Jolson in Warner Brothers' *The Jazz Singer* in 1927. The previous year, Warner Brothers had produced a film with synchronized music recorded on discs—a system called Vitaphone. Before, silent movies had been accompanied by the movie-house piano or organ, the player changing the music's rhythm and mood to suit the action on-screen. But with the arrival of "talkies," dialogue took the place of both the piano and the exaggerated gestures, costumes, and sets of the silent movies. The story no longer depended on fast-moving slapstick and caricature, whether in Felix the Cat cartoons or the comedies of Fatty Arbuckle or the clownish but sad Charlie Chaplin.

body and snakeskin upholstery exactly matching the color of her skin. The effect of her dramatic entrance was captured in *Vogue*:

"She had come in without a wrap, and the length of her graceful body … is swathed in a full blue tulle frock with a bodice of blue snakeskin…. Her hair, which naturally grows in tight curls, is plastered close to her head with black shellac. As she appears at the Folies Bergères, she wears only a diamanté maillot of tulle and red gloves with diamond balls hanging from the tips of her fingers; the effect is up to the wildest imagination of Beardsley" [a British artist known for bizarre artwork].

In New York City's Harlem, white society frequented the jazz clubs, where great musicians like Louis Armstrong, Duke Ellington, and Cab Calloway entertained. The most famous of these spots was the Cotton Club. This personal memory of Sonny Greer conjures up the atmosphere of the late twenties:

"We went to work at 11 o'clock at night, and nobody knew when closing hour was. We usually didn't get through till seven or eight in the morning, but it was beautiful … all kinds of people mixed there—show people, socialites, debutantes, musicians, and racketeers—and everybody had a lovely time. It was still Prohibition … nobody could get a drink of booze in the place unless I gave an okay…. The last show at the Cotton Club went on at two and the club closed at 3:30 or four. Then everybody would go next door … or to the breakfast dance at Small's Paradise, where the floor show went on at 6 o'clock in the morning."

Sometimes black musicians were hired to play in private Manhattan apartments or country homes, but color barriers were rigidly kept, and white and

▶It was very fashionable for white jazz fans to be seen at the Cotton Club, one of the few places where they and African Americans could mix with any degree of ease.

◄ Novelty acts were very popular. Here the almost identical Hungarian Dolly Sisters are seen performing at London's exclusive Kit Kat Club.

►The vamp, with her kohl-rimmed eyes, exotic Egyptian dress, and orientalist interior decor, is a typical figure of the twenties.

The Wall Street Crash

In October 1929, virtually overnight, the fortunes of many Americans just getting used to their massive spending power, came crashing down. Big profits led to wild speculation, causing the prices of stock shares to rise above their true value. The resulting "slump" and panic were inevitable. The dramatic fall in prices affected the rest of the world's stocks and shares and led to large scale unemployment. The economic crisis generated an air of seriousness and "playing it safe" at the end of the decade. And as if fashion were reflecting the stock market crash, the hemlines of women's dresses also dropped.

black audiences did not mix. Though jazz was thought of as an expression of black culture, white American jazz bands also attracted huge crowds—for instance, the Original Dixieland Band and Paul Whiteman, whose orchestra was the first to perform *Rhapsody in Blue* in 1924, with the composer George Gershwin at the piano.

►The Wall Street Crash wrecked businesses and thousands of ordinary lives in a matter of days. Many suicides were reported among those who simply could not face the shame of bankruptcy.

$100 WILL
BUY THIS CAR
MUST HAVE CASH
LOST ALL ON THE
STOCK MARKET

Flappers

Thoroughly Modern Millies

Undeterred by the disapproval of adults, the younger generation was setting out to have a good time. The emancipated female painted her face and drank cocktails. She smoked cigarettes in elegant holders. She might wear a Turkish-inspired "smoking suit" and turban. Her boyish silhouette is sometimes referred to as the *garçonne* look—all flat-chested beneath the new shapeless fit and revolutionary brassiere. To achieve the new slim line—modern, minimal, geometric—the surface of the body was broken up by shapes of contrasting color, dismantled, and reassembled rather like a Cubist painting by Picasso or Braque.

By 1925, dresses were the shortest in history—an act of the devil, some thought. There was an international outcry to protect the moral code; campaigns were launched to save the future generation from chaos and destruction. What's more, flesh-colored stockings of artificial silk—which women of all income levels could afford—gave legs the impression of nudity. Within the United States, Ohio and Utah responded by passing laws fixing hems at about seven inches from the floor.

▶"Oxford bags," made popular in the summer of 1925 by young university undergraduates, were soon taken up by other fashion-conscious men about town.

▼ A young, independent woman taking it easy in a smoking suit in 1922. The texture of the fur ankle trim combines luxuriously with the luminous surface of the artificial silk textile. The cigarette holder and turban add to the exotic effect and were no doubt thought appropriate for the smoking of Turkish or Egyptian cigarettes.

▲ "That skirt's so short you can see your stocking tops!" If he thinks this is accidental, the young man is missing the point. As skirts became shorter, garters—embroidered, beaded, and definitely intended to be seen—also became popular.

Color and Form

For much of the decade, dresses and sweaters were pure rectangles—like canvases waiting to be painted. Several artists did become involved in dress and textile design. In Paris, Sonia Delaunay created colorful abstract compositions in fabric and fur. Collaborating with furrier Jacques Heim, she made a coat and matching seat upholstery for her brightly painted Citroën sports car. In Vienna, members of the Wiener Werkstätte (Viennese craft workshops) created fascinating stylized floral decorations for hats out of sculpted and sewn pieces of felt, along with innovative cloth necklaces. Soviet artists designed nothing so frivolous or decorative: the painters Popova and Stepanova applied Constructivist principles to everyday dresses, making dynamic use of red.

Opposition in Dress

Just as hemlines rose, the emphasis on women's legs was matched by the voluminous dimensions of "Oxford bags." These broad trousers, worn by undergraduates of Oxford

University, were a cool—but disheveled—response to the hot British summer of 1925. Looking back on his own experiences as an Oxford undergraduate at that time, British aesthete (admirer of beauty) Harold Acton described these trousers as a localized Victorian Revival, worn with "high-necked jumpers [sweaters] of all tints and textures." In America, Ivy League undergraduates in the Northeast enjoyed a relaxed mood in dress—blazers and flannel trousers, ascots rather than ties—that broke away from the conventions of the three-piece suit. Less prestigious American colleges saw their men adopting sharp-brimmed hats, raccoon fur coats, and two-toned "saddle shoes." Fraternities flourished, each identified by a particular code of dress.

Before World War I, color, texture, looser and lighter-weight clothes had gone hand in hand with progressive thinking. In his bohemian days, American poet Ezra Pound had worn a green jacket trimmed with glass buttons. In the twenties, such elements gradually entered mainstream fashion. Young men's clothes were very colorful compared to the khaki and gray of their parents. They wore lounge suits with jackets when in town instead of knee-length frock coats, and their trousers were creased front and back and turned up at the ankle, while conservative dressers stayed with side creases and straight legs of narrower cut. New men about town were clean shaven instead of bearded.

Short Back and Sides

One of the most persistent features of the twenties was the cloche hat, worn by women to tea dances, in the street, and even at lunch parties in their own homes. This head-hugging hat was as storm-proof as a flying helmet. It necessitated a short hairstyle called a bob, a shingle, or an Eton crop. Before the decade had run its course, 99 percent of the American and Western European female population had their hair cut short.

▲Another glimpse of stocking: Miss Kitty Lee, society girl of Baltimore, Maryland, with a portrait of her boyfriend printed onto her stockings. She has also had her hair bobbed.

▼These cloche hats carry coded love symbols. For the initiated, tying the ribbon in an arrow-like way indicated a single girl who had already given her promise of love, while the firm knot meant she was married—and a flirtatious bow signaled the independent, fancy-free girl.

The heroine of F. Scott Fitzgerald's short story of 1920, "Bernice Bobs Her Hair," fascinates her friends at parties by talking of bobbing her hair. When she actually strides into a barber's and has it done, she is immediately rejected by her horrified young companions for looking so ugly.

Simply Shocking!

One of the "madcap" ideas of the bright young people was to crash parties—and there were plenty of them. Everyone enjoyed song and dance and dressing up. In the United States, the "Jazz Babies" were fascinated by scavenger hunts. But the twenties were a time when shock and outrage were touched off far more easily than today. A scarlet, backless evening gown was enough to do the trick.

▼"For those who instinctively seek a quality product"—to match their quality clothes. This Chevrolet advertisement was featured in American *Vogue*, 1929.

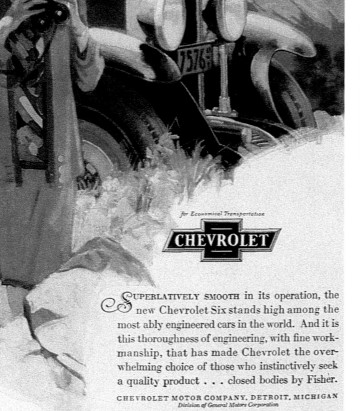

for Economical Transportation

CHEVROLET

$\mathbf{S}$UPERLATIVELY SMOOTH in its operation, the new Chevrolet Six stands high among the most ably engineered cars in the world. And it is this thoroughness of engineering, with fine workmanship, that has made Chevrolet the overwhelming choice of those who instinctively seek a quality product . . . closed bodies by Fisher.

CHEVROLET MOTOR COMPANY, DETROIT, MICHIGAN
Division of General Motors Corporation

The Roadster, $525; The Phaeton, $525; The Coach, $595; The Coupe, $595; The Sedan, $675; The Sport Cabriolet, $695; The Convertible Landau, $725. All prices f. o. b. factory, Flint, Michigan

▲A youthful party in Paris, from *Art Goût Beauté,* Christmas issue, 1923. The young men's formal attire is softened and given a rather bohemian look by large, floppy, black bow ties. The four women in the foreground wear evening gowns by the Paris fashion houses of (left to right) Molyneux, Phillippe et Gaston, Lucien Lelong, and Bernard.

The Perfect Gentleman

American Dreams

As travel became easier, transatlantic exchanges of ideas were frequent. Novelist F. Scott Fitzgerald's high-living, high-spending Jay Gatsby, in the novel *The Great Gatsby*, embodied the aspirations of those men for whom success was synonymous with good dress. As Gatsby opened "two hulking patent cabinets which held his massed suits and dressing gowns and ties, and his shirts, piled like bricks in stacks a dozen high," he explained that a man in England sent him clothes every season, spring and fall. His admirers looked on in amazement as he pulled out shirts "of sheer linen and thick silk and fine flannel … and the soft rich pile mounted higher —shirts with stripes and scrolls and plaids in coral and apple-green and lavender and faint orange, with monograms in Indian blue."

▲Al Capone believed that being a gangster was no excuse for looking less than your best, especially when you were likely to be on the front page of the newspapers.

In New York, the Brooks Brothers men's store was the place to go for traditional dressing. Meanwhile, in Chicago, the press reported on gangster Al "Scarface" Capone, who paid attention to detail in everything he touched. That included his spats, his showy necktie, his fob watch and chain tucked into a vest pocket, his distinctive pin-striped suits—and, of course, the brimmed felt hat worn at an angle designed to cast a shadow over the scar on his cheek.

Prince of Wales Checks

London's Bond Street and Savile Row led the world in men's fashion, and their greatest ambassador was Edward, Prince of Wales, heir to the British throne. He much admired the casual style of Americans, and whenever he could, he introduced elements of sportswear and country clothing into his own dapper wardrobe. He loved fast cars and horseback riding, preferring the ease of a knitted sleeveless pullover sweater to a tailored vest beneath his hunting coat. In 1922, when playing golf at St. Andrews, Scotland, he sported a brightly knitted Fair Isle pullover sweater—worn with plus fours, also known as knickers. This attracted public attention and became a best seller, drawing in many orders for the Scottish island knitters. *Vanity Fair* magazine regularly featured the Prince of Wales in its "Well-Dressed Man" column.

▼When the Prince of Wales wore a Fair Isle pullover sweater with knickers for playing golf, he started a fashion for this Scottish knitwear almost overnight.

▲ Gentlemen would never fail to raise their hats to passing acquaintances in a park. The suit, worn with double-breasted vest and double-breasted overcoat, is by French tailors Lus and Befue, 1922.

▲German advertisement for Kaloderma shaving cream, 1929. The stiff-winged collar, white bow tie, and white pointed vest are all features of the most formal, conventional evening dress for men—worn with top hat and tails.

◄ Colorful printed silk fashions by Sulka, for men with dash and cash. Accessories like these poured out of Jay Gatsby's wardrobe in *The Great Gatsby.*

◄ A fashionable French couple walking in the Bois de Boulogne, Paris, 1921. With great flair, the man wears a striped shirt with plain white collar (detachable), tweed jacket, pin-striped pants, and spats—an unconventional combination that no American or British man would ever have dreamed of.

▲Rudolph Valentino, perfectly made up and with slicked-back hair, was the heartthrob of the silent screen—and one of Hollywood's best-dressed men—until his tragically early death in 1926.

Getting It Right

Despite the liberalism of the day, a strict sense of etiquette still taught a young man what was permissible and "correct." No "gentleman" ever showed his suspenders or shirtsleeves. Nor would he mismatch a hat and coat—Homburgs and straw hats should not be worn with evening dress, whereas caps belonged to work wear and sports clothing. The gestures that went with them—raising hats and doffing caps—were signs of social distinction, especially in Europe, where class and social conventions were more clearly defined than in the United States.

"Stop Flirting"

American dancer Fred Astaire was a huge stage success in 1923 when he made his first London appearance in *Stop Flirting*. When the Prince of Wales visited him backstage, Astaire was impressed: "HRH was unquestionably the best-dressed young man in the world, and I was missing none of it. I noted particularly the white waistcoat lapels—his own special type. This waistcoat did not show below the dress coat front. I liked that."

The following morning, Astaire paid a visit to Hawkes and Curtis, shirt and waistcoat makers "By Appointment to the Prince". The royal outfitters, however, ruthlessly protected their clients, and the world's hottest new dancing star was politely turned away from Hawkes and Curtis and had to go elsewhere to follow the best-dressed man's style.

◄ **Fred Astaire was never less than perfectly turned out, on-screen or off.**

Stars of Stage and Screen

Sparkle and Glamour

Motion pictures began life as an inexpensive form of escapism, available to a far wider audience than the theater or ballet. In terms of dress, the medium had immense power—especially in the silent early years, when sharply defined costumes and gestures were essential to the narrative. Black-and-white movies called for strong tonal contrasts in the clothes worn by the stars; the sparkle of beads and metallic finishes and the movement and texture of feathers could all be picked up by the camera to dramatic effect.

Onstage, too, the quality of light made people look at color in a different way. In 1927, the British menswear trade journal *Tailor and Cutter* noted its approval of the midnight blue evening suit worn by Jack Buchanan, the star of André Charlot's revue *A to Z,* because it looked much better under electric light than did conventional black. Buchanan also had the ideal physique to promote the broad-shouldered suit introduced by Savile Row in 1925.

The film heroes of the decade appeared as smooth and unblemished as the female stars since the negatives were touched up to perfection. Rudolph Valentino—labeled "The Sheik" after one film in which he played a romantic desert prince—caused women to swoon in their seats, though to our eyes, he may appear rather camp. On the other hand, US Olympic gold swimmer Johnny Weissmuller, alias Tarzan, flexed his muscles with great charisma—although even he would begin to look unreal compared to the authentically clothed cowboys like Gary Cooper, who first appeared in the thirties.

Vamps, Virgins, and Femmes Fatales

Recently described as the forerunner of today's well-tailored woman, Louise Brooks's independent, tomboyish style matched the office dresses and suits she wore in films. These widely influenced the viewing public. Lillian Gish, on the other hand, was always cast as the pure maiden—dressed inevitably in white, her sugary-sweet image was not a fashion sensation.

The vamp, exemplified by stars like the hypnotic and seductive Theda Bara, whose eyelids glistened with Vaseline, was another female type that had entered the movies during World War I. Titles like *Sinners in Silk* took the opportunity to show off "prostitute pink" teddies of silk or rayon. Among the other femmes fatales to be "discovered" by German and American film directors were Pola Negri, Gloria Swanson, the great Greta Garbo, and Clara Bow, known as the "It Girl." "It" meant sex appeal. An American dress fabric, printed all over with the word *it*, was designed by Ruzzie Green in 1928.

Not all of these stars wore silk pajamas—but those who did were generally considered "fast," that is, of loose morals. In the Gershwin musical comedy *Oh, Kay!,* which opened on Broadway in 1926, the English star Gertrude Lawrence wore such an outfit. The silk was encrusted with pearls and the matching open

▶Sultry Vilma Banky makes the most of her gypsy looks as the cover girl of *The Picturegoer*, November 1926. These magazines had an enormous influence on fashion as hopeful young women did their best to imitate the frocks and hairdos of their heroines, hoping a little of that romance would rub off on them.

THE NOVEMBER

Picturegoer

MONTHLY

1926

Vol. 12
No. 71

1/- net

Vilma Banky
SPECIAL
ARTICLE
INSIDE

robe seductively trimmed with ostrich plumes, which wafted from the sleeves. For her stage and film appearances, she was dressed by the Paris House of Molyneux free of charge because the publicity for them was invaluable. In France, another star of musical comedy, Yvonne Printemps, wore Jeanne Lanvin garden party dresses and picture hats—very romantic and escapist in the age of the machine and the tubular cut.

▲Greta Garbo always managed to look mysterious and a little melancholy, even when wearing fairly ordinary street clothes.

Hollywood Clothes Horses

By the end of the twenties, the movie industry was centered on Hollywood, and the silver screen became the means of spreading glamorous fashion trends. The response of the Paris couturiers was to hire American models to show their collections every autumn and spring. Several couturiers also designed for the movies. Hollywood designers Howard Greer and Travis Branton had worked in the fashion business before entering the film industry and knew what was photogenic. On the other hand, Coco Chanel's ballet costumes may have been superb onstage, but her garments were too understated to make an impact on-screen. Shoe designer Salvatore Ferragamo first attracted fashionable customers by making sandals for the film, *The Ten Commandments* (1924). Paris and Hollywood had all the makings of a perfect alliance.

▲ American film star Clara Bow, with her trademark kohl-rimmed eyes and cupid-bow lips, was christened the "It" girl. "It" was polite shorthand for sex appeal, and she certainly had it.

►Louise Brooks in one of the typical softly tailored outfits that, while appealingly tomboyish, left no doubt as to her femininity.

Chic Parisienne

Great Couturiers

Throughout the twenties, the well-established fashion houses, such as Callot Soeurs, Jacques Doucet, Lucile (Lady Duff Gordon), Paul Poiret, and Worth, continued to create exciting garments, heavily embroidered and intricately constructed from beautiful fabrics. However, Coco Chanel, Madeleine Vionnet, and Elsa Schiaparelli broke new ground in the cut and concept of clothes, responding through their designs to broader movements in modern art.

◄ Rich silks, black-and-white embroidery, and monkey-fur collar trim combine in this evening gown and cape designed by Paul Poiret.

▲Designer Paul Poiret and his tailor put the finishing touches to a model dress worn by a "mannequin."

▲"What! Already dressed?" This evening gown and silk pajama outfit, both by Jeanne Lanvin, show contrasting styles.

▼The perfect accessories: a sleek, diamanté-studded shoe designed by Pérugia and long ropes of pearls. Sometimes looped into a knot, these were draped seductively to draw attention to bare, suntanned skin.

Rich Little Poor Girl

Chanel combined simplicity with elegance. Impressed by work clothes and the comfort of men's cardigan sweaters worn by the women who took over men's jobs in the factories during World War I, she favored rough tweeds and other workwear fabrics, making it fashionable to look poor. She also devised dresses and two-piece outfits made from Rodier's wool jersey. Her collections featured numerous variations on the sweater theme for day wear. Many of her geometric designs were inspired by Scottish Fair Isle and Icelandic knitting, with their jigsaws of pattern and color. The little black dress and edge-to-edge coat (in which side fronts meet, with no fastening or overlap) are also attributed to her. She also pioneered the wearing of frankly fake jewelry, including long ropes of artificial pearls.

The Art of Deception

Chanel's greatest rival was Italian-born Elsa Schiaparelli, famous for the incongruous elements she introduced into her designs. Schiaparelli was much influenced by Salvador Dalí and the Surrealist movement. To her, dress designing was not a profession but an art, which should always treat the body like an architectural frame, with respect. Yet she was frustrated by the force of fashion because many of her original ideas were copied in mass production. In her

autobiography *Shocking Pink,* she wrote: "As soon as a dress is born it has already become a thing of the past…. A dress cannot just hang like a painting on the wall, or like a book remain intact and live a long and sheltered life."

Schiaparelli's clothes were always expensive, beautifully cut, and incredibly chic—but whimsical. Around 1926, her first fashion hit was a trompe l'oeil (literally, "fool the eye") sweater with the image of a huge bow hand-knitted into the design. The garment finished at the natural waist, in complete contrast to the straight, tubular, hip-hugging silhouette of the time. Immediately, a buyer from the New York store Strauss ordered forty, with matching skirts. This success led to many more deceptive sweaters—designs taken from artifacts of the Congo, a knitted simulation of a sailor's chest tattooed with pierced hearts and snakes and a skeleton of white ribs against a black background. Schiaparelli also produced silk ties printed with a montage of fake newspaper clippings all about herself—one of the first puns on the "designer label" idea. Schiaparelli's exciting color sense—particularly her trademark "shocking" pink—found expression in a whole range of fashion accessories, and she experimented with new cloths, textures, and finishes, producing white rubberized crepe for women's flying outfits in 1928.

On the Bias

Most of the tube-shaped dresses followed the straight grain of the fabric. Madeleine Vionnet's inventive clothes, however, were cut on the bias from the shoulders and hips using heavy satin and crepe, giving them a fluid and perfectly sculpted look. The cut gave the garment a built-in elasticity: her low-backed evening dresses stayed in place with no hooks, ties, or other fastenings. In addition to long evening gowns in understated tones of oyster and pastel blue and other draped dresses for wearing in the afternoon, she designed tailored suits and capes for outdoor wear. Like Chanel, Vionnet never sketched her designs but always worked in three dimensions, letting the fabric dictate, preferring tucks to cuts. She draped the cloth around a wooden model a quarter of human size, which stood on a revolving piano stool.

◄ **This evening gown of heavy silk satin with a low, draped back was designed by Madeleine Vionnet in about 1924.**

▲Some events—like the Paris Grand Prix of 1924—have always encouraged the extremes of fashion. There are spots ...

▶...and spots, as in the restrained elegance of this day dress, with its dropped sash-waist.

▲Josephine Baker, despite her half-naked "primitive" stage routines, was an elegant and beautiful woman and was dressed by many of the top designers, including Poiret.

Boutiques and Branches

Several new names sprang up in the course of the decade, and although Paris remained the center of high fashion, the whole scene diversified, becoming more international. American Hattie Carnegie, who had launched her first collection in 1918, added ready-to-wear models ten years later, following the footsteps of Paris's Lucien Lelong. Several designers opened boutiques in fashionable resorts, targeting their garments at a specific clientele and lending their names to perfumes, as Paul Poiret had begun to do just before World War I. Schiaparelli led the field in creating colorful accessories—handbags, shoes, and even wigs for skiing—to match her outfits. And in 1926, Jeanne Lanvin opened the first boutique for men to complement her clothes for women and children.

Tutmania and All That Jazz

Tutmania

In 1922, British archaeologist Howard Carter discovered the tomb of the ancient Egyptian boy-king Tutankhamen, filled with treasures buried for 3,000 years. The excavations remained shrouded in secrecy until the following year, but by then the world was spinning into a frenzy of "Tutmania." Egyptian motifs were everywhere. Cheney Brothers, the American textile company that produced stylish hand-printed dress silks, sent out a designer to Egypt to seek firsthand inspiration. Hieroglyphs and motifs that looked like a cross between an Art Deco sunburst and Cleopatra's headdress covered fashion accessories, from handbags to enameled cigarette holders and even "mummy" powder compacts. Ancient Egypt lived again in cheap imitations of "Cleo" earrings and scarab-shaped jewelry, while the lotus motif became the logo of a brand of footwear.

North Africa also influenced fashion, but in a more general sense. Black cotton net stoles from Morocco, decorated with twisted strips of silver arranged in geometric patterns, were popular in this period. They created the sort of dazzle that black-and-white movies encouraged. Women bathed their bodies in iodine baths to tint the skin a reddish color. Brilliantly offset by this effect or by a tan, ropes of pearls looked stunning. Many women used kohl as eyeliner to accentuate the eyes in a vampish manner.

▲ Egyptian influences and motifs are clear in these elegant dresses.

▲Walpole were right on top of the news with this smart overblouse of 1923, incorporating panels of embroidery in Egyptian-inspired hieroglyphic patterns.

Rhythms and Patterns of Jazz

The jerky and syncopated rhythms of jazz and dances like the Black Bottom and the Charleston were echoed in the hard-edged patterns of dress fabrics. Corsetless flappers moved freely on the dance floor, and their loose-cut dresses, heavily decorated with glass beads, swirled around them, fringes swinging wildly, dazzling brilliantly under sharp electric light.

▲British designer Norman Hartnell, favorite of the royal family, created this evening gown for the 1924 season. Its hint of the exotic is in the metal bead embroidery and ostrich plumes.

45

▲"Visit Egypt!" cried British *Vogue* in October 1929, promising twenty-eight days of luxurious travel for only seventy-two pounds, ten shillings (about $350).

"Primitivism"

The "primitive" appealed to the new machine-driven, urbanized world. As a result, the competitive mass-produced world of fashion borrowed a rich variety of decorative motifs from many cultures. These included the rhythmic stepped patterns of South America's pre-Columbian ceramics and tapestries, stylized floral borders of East European folk embroidery, and the triangles of West African cloths. Batik was also in fashion—and had the advantage of being simple to experiment with at home, especially for those women who got hold of a manual on the craft by artist Jessie M. King (1922) called *How Cinderella Went to the Ball*. French painter Raoul Dufy designed hundreds of textiles for the Lyons silk firm Bianchini-Férier, many taking the theme of the jungle and other exotic images.

Fashions for the Orient

The impact of the *Thousand and One Nights*, popularized in Paris by Diaghilev's Russian Ballet production of *Schéhérazade* in 1910, continued to resound well into the twenties—especially in the field of color and the rich textures of Turkish velvet and brocade. Although Paul Poiret's turbans and pantaloon gowns had faded from fashion, the love for Oriental styles lived on in classic styles. Historic and exotic themes were interpreted in a very individual way by Mariano Fortuny, the Venice-based dress and textile designer.

The creations of the Callot Soeurs (of Russian ancestry) were covered in lavish Chinese-style embroideries worked into birds of paradise and lotus flowers in the colors of painted porcelain. The skills of their needlewomen also created tassels, scallops, and lavish beading around the knee-length hems, drawing attention to the legs. Japanese style, too, was popular; the decoration of T-shaped kimonos was easily translated into peasant-inspired Art Deco coats, overlaid with apple blossoms, bamboo, and mythical phoenixes.

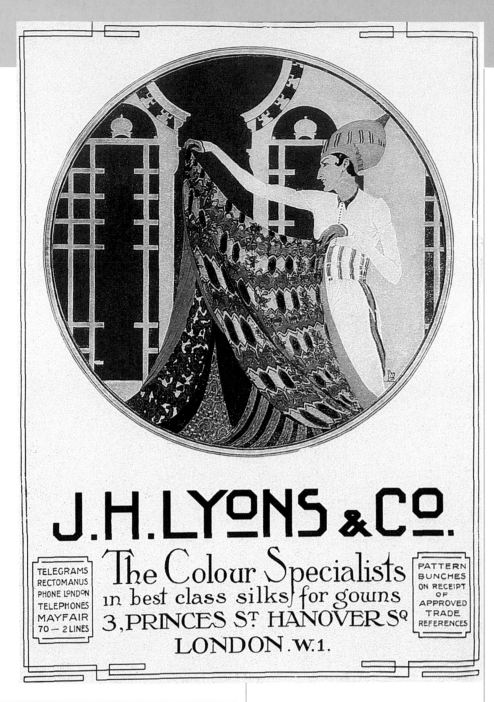

J.H. LYONS & CO.

The Colour Specialists in best class silks for gowns 3, PRINCES ST. HANOVER SQ. LONDON .w.1.

TELEGRAMS RECTOMANUS PHONE LONDON TELEPHONES MAYFAIR 70 — 2 LINES

PATTERN BUNCHES ON RECEIPT OF APPROVED TRADE REFERENCES

▲A German silver-and-cloisonné enamel scarab brooch of the 1920s. The scarab beetle was sacred to the ancient Egyptians, its image appearing frequently in Egyptian art and on jewelry.

◀This advertisement for the colorful silk fabrics of Lyons and Company promises all the mystery of the Arabian bazaar, to be enjoyed in the safety of London's West End.

▲One of Léon Bakst's typically exotic costumes for the ballet Le Dieu Bleu, which had taken Europe by storm in 1912.

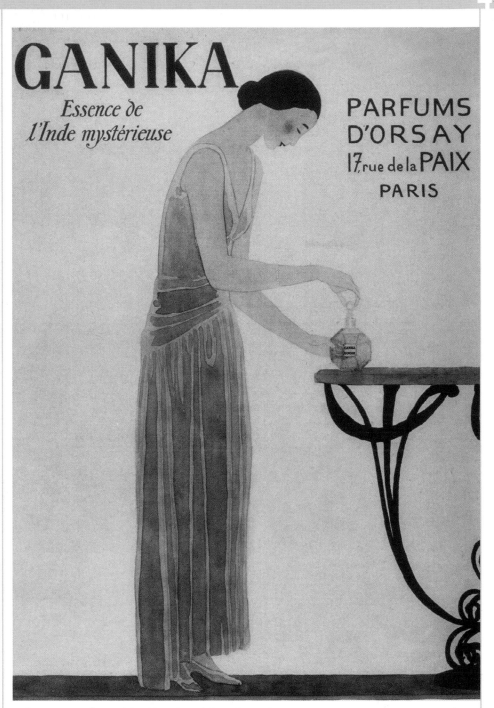

▲Similarly, perfume with a hint of sandalwood or spices could conjure up the exoticism of India. The bottle, too, is a fine example of Art Deco design.

Skin Deep

The Cosmetic Industry Gets a Face-lift

The makeup industry and beauty parlors had originally based their offerings on a range of face creams and beauty products to improve the skin. These were the products on which the empires of America's Elizabeth Arden and Helena Rubinstein were built in the early years of the twentieth century. But in the twenties, the distinction between natural and artificial became blurred. Plucked eyebrows, rouge, and lipstick expressed both femininity and female emancipation. By 1929, a cosmetic advertisement in the *Ladies' Home Journal* confidently claimed: "the alluring note of scarlet will stay with you for hours."

Before World War I, such enhancements to beauty had signified loose morals, but as the twenties progressed, obviously applied cosmetics on faces highlighted by black kohl-rimmed eyes and primary red lips became accepted symbols of the new age. Makeup was synonymous with emancipation—and a beautiful, slender body and easy-fitting, lightweight clothes set the standard of feminine beauty. Published at the end of the decade, Helena Rubinstein's *The Art of Feminine Beauty* proclaimed that women were entitled to good looks and independence.

Black Beauty

While white women were busy working up a suntan, black women were treating their faces with various skin-whitening potions. A leading figure in this business was Madame C. J. Walker, America's first black millionaire, whose hair-relaxing system became the staple offering of her highly successful black beauty parlors and the Walker College of Hair Culture.

By the time of the disastrous Wall Street Crash in October 1929, American women were spending $750 million a year on face makeup.

Barely Visible

This kind of skin- and body-consciousness was also expressed in new fibers and light fabrics. "Art" (artificial) silk—a man-made fiber made from plant cellulose, variously termed acetate or viscose rayon—was first developed in the late nineteenth century, but after World War I, when acetate was used to coat the canvas wings of aircraft, this inexpensive simulation of silk was produced commercially. As the decade progressed, production increased; in the United States, production of viscose rayon rose from 8 million pounds in 1920 to 53 million in 1925.

Both acetate and viscose rayon were naturally more lustrous than real silk and had a brightening effect when woven into gaily colored motifs for women's dresses. But the biggest impact of these new fibers lay in the production of flesh-colored stockings (to be superseded by nylon from 1940), which simulated bare legs. This was a stark contrast with old-fashioned black wool stockings, especially when the hemlines rose. And what's more, working girls could afford them.

▲McCallum's silk hosiery, advertised in American *Vogue*, December 1921.

▲Strong, light, and practical "Hercules" roller-printed cotton, manufactured by the Joshua Hoyle Company of Manchester, England.

▲Models parade a selection of new corsetry at Dorothy Perkins's Oxford Street shop in London, May 1925. Girdles and one-piece models are on display here, both of which were gradually replaced by the lighter-weight versions.

Lighter Clothing

The general effect was to create far less bulky garments. Between the outbreak of World War I and 1928, the quality of fabric invested in a woman's complete "costume" (as a whole outfit was then called) was reduced from nineteen yards to seven. And thanks to "art silk," the fabric was lighter in weight. Underwear, too, was modernized as linen or cambric panties, and tight-laced corsets worn over camisoles were abandoned in favor of flesh-colored brassieres and cami-knickers—an all-in-one garment combining camisole and panties.

In Search of Sun and Sport

Elasticity in Action

One of the biggest influences on fashion has been sport. In the 1920s, barriers were broken down between these two fields of dress. Coco Chanel revolutionized day wear and sportswear alike by creating casual suits and golfing outfits of jersey that had "elasticity in action" and "slender lines in repose."

Since golf fell into the category of traditional sports, golf clothing, like that for riding and fishing, tended to be made of old-fashioned heavier cloths, such as tweed and plaid. The conservative nature of the fabric was echoed by the restrained cut of the golfing skirt—inverted pleats that did not swing around the body so widely that they made the wearer off balance.

Skiing and flying, which belonged to the new generation of sports, demanded flashy metallic detail, dazzling snow white, or the nearest thing to primary colors. Waterproof yet pliable ski mittens were made of chromed (leather with a metallic finish) horsehide. Buckles and zippers were used experimentally as outer details on garments whose component parts could be detached and rearranged to perform a new function and create a new garment within seconds. For example, in 1926, the house of Redfern, an established producer of yachting wear, designed a white velvet skating outfit whose skirt zipped off to become a scarf.

Tennis, Anyone?

Wimbledon's Centre Court was the focal point of radical sportswear that hit the headlines, both on the court and off. Male players still wore long trousers and shirts for tennis, but in 1926, the Duke of York set a precedent at the Lawn Tennis Championships by wearing "sleeves cut short above the elbow." From then on, "no other man need be afraid to do so," assured the Sunlight League's Dr. Caleb Saleeby.

▼Winter sports clothing in "agnella," a woven wool fabric resembling sheepskin, designed by Rodier.

▲In this fashionable golfing party, the clothes illustrate the trend toward looser, less bulky styles for outdoor activities. Note the "Prince of Wales" Fair Isle sweater.

Materials
from
Hercules

65   66   67

SPORT
AND PLAY IN COLOURED
PRINTS

▲Smart, simple casual styles in lightweight printed fabrics allowed women to feel they were part of the sporty set, even if they were only there as spectators.

▲French tennis star Suzanne Lenglen sports a Jean Patou outfit at the Wimbledon lawn tennis championships. Her "short" skirts shocked crowds in 1922, and she was obliged to wear stockings to preserve her modesty.

▶Sportswear for the beach, on sale in the Paris department store Les Grands Magasins du Louvre in 1929. The influence of Coco Chanel is felt strongly in these outfits, especially the three-piece suit with geometric-patterned sweater.

French women's champion Suzanne Lenglen caused a sensation with her chic wardrobe of tennis dresses designed by Jean Patou. She was instantly recognizable by the colored bandeau wound around her head, matching her monogrammed sleeveless cardigan. The low-cut neckline of the dress featured an ingenious lapel that could be buttoned up to the neck after the match.

Another tennis star who attracted imitators was America's Helen Wills, famous for her eyeshade. Together, she and Lenglen changed the face of tennis since their less restrictive clothes helped to speed up the game. Nevertheless, modesty and convention demanded that they continue to wear white stockings—baring the legs was a freedom and privilege as yet restricted to the seaside resort.

▲ A carefree beach dress in chevron-patterned lightweight wool by the great French textile designer-manufacturer of the decade, Paul Rodier.

▲Jane Régny clothes for yachting, 1928. The suit of white serge unbuttons to reveal a slinky white jersey bathing costume underneath, embroidered on the pocket with the "JR" monogram.

From Riviera to Palm Beach

A suntan was once the rough-and-ready sign of a peasant worker, but during the twenties, it acquired a sense of refinement. Those who had sufficient wealth and time on their hands to travel abroad paraded the decks of their yachts or the esplanades of the new seaside resorts. The pages of *Vogue* featured the Palm Beach and Riviera styles—beach trousers and backless bathing suits. These originated in the Paris couture houses but could be bought in the growing number of boutiques catering to this leisured outdoor life under the sun. Charles Worth opened boutiques at Biarritz and Cannes, two of France's most fashionable resorts, and in the United States, the West Coast had become a center for outdoor fashion by the late 1920s.

British photographer and fashion chronicler Cecil Beaton recalled the personification of "a new type of woman" in the beautiful form of a Spanish duchess: "wearing a short white tunic with a deep scooped neckline and a skirt that stretched hardly to the knees. She wore sunburn stockings with white satin shoes whose Spanish spike heels were fully six inches high…. She was burned by the sun to a deep shade of iodine. Two enormous rows of pearl teeth were bared in a white, vital grin, complementing the half a dozen rows of pearls as large as pigeon's eggs that hung about her neck."

▶As transportation improved, the seaside offered relaxation and sport for all, not just the rich—although you still had to have the right clothes.

▼Bathing beauties under a sunshade inspired by the artist Dufy. Disappointingly, this glamorous "beach" scene was, in fact, a posed studio shot.

HEFT 17 ZWEITES MAIHEFT 1927

DIE DAME

VERLAG
ULLSTEIN
BERLIN

◄ Advertisers and magazines were quick to cash in on the appeal of sport and the longing of towndwellers for the country life.

Alternative Dressing

Bohemian Alternatives

Those in revolt against the upper-class "boiled shirts" (linen shirts with starched, stiff collars and cuffs) chose historicism, exoticism, peasant clothing, or work wear as an anti-fashion statement. Individually, members of avant-garde London's Bloomsbury and Chelsea sets selected one or a combination of these alternatives. The painter Vanessa Bell, sister of writer Virginia Woolf, favored strong shades of purple and vermilion and rummaged around the markets of Europe for old fabrics and costumes. Artist Walter Sickert, then in his sixties, dressed in loud, large-checked suits with a white bowler hat, while fellow artist Duncan Grant chose working dress in slightly quieter hues—a loose-fitting tweed jacket, open-necked shirt with bandana, and corduroy trousers. Artistic women wore gypsy-type clothes, dirndl skirts with nipped-in waists, and head scarves instead of the more formal hat.

New York's Greenwich Village bohemians also went about hatless, and some individuals were especially eccentric. The writer Djuna Barnes was instantly recognizable by her dramatic black cloak, while a woman calling herself Baronin von Freytag-von-Loringhoven took everything to extremes by wearing black lipstick and yellow face powder and shaving her head.

◀ Programs of dress reform and female emancipation often resulted in rather mannish outfits.

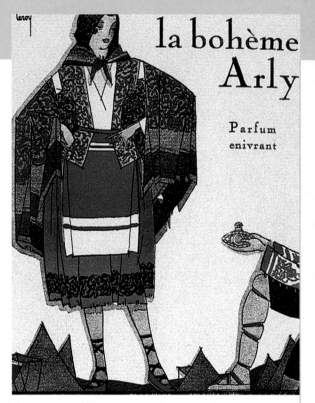

▲The costume of peasants in eastern Europe and Scandinavia was the inspiration for many alternative dressers, who hoped perfume would release their bohemian nature.

▼Half-Arab, half-nun: the eccentric Lady Dorothy Mills, novelist and traveler, on the cover of *The Tatler* in January 1923.

◄ Unisex clothing on the streets of Reedy, West Virginia—but only after a referendum had been held in the town as to whether women could be seen in knickers.

Raymond Duncan, brother of barefoot dancer Isadora, founded a school for the study of Greek arts and crafts in Neuilly, Paris, where he lived collectively in a vegetarian colony and wore handwoven cloths based on Greek vase paintings. A visitor in 1928 described him as "neat … with his long hair pinned in silky braids in a crown around his small, eagle-like head. One end of his elegant tunic was flung across his left shoulder, and his bare feet, in the simplest of thonged sandals, were immaculately clean…. He spoke with the flat twang of a mid-west farmer."

Cross-dressing

Before World War I, aesthetic figures like Oscar Wilde and Rupert Brooke had expressed their independence from the Establishment by wearing more color and softening the silhouette of their clothes. They wore soft turn-down collars and enormous ties. In the twenties, playwright and songwriter Noel Coward indulged in "a long suppressed desire for silk pyjamas and underclothes" after the roaring success of his first play, *The Vortex*, in 1924. He also took to wearing "coloured turtle-neck jerseys, actually more for comfort than for effect, and soon I [Coward] was informed by my evening paper that I had started a fashion."

While men pampered themselves and softened up their wardrobes, some women went for a harsher look.

◄ Fashionably flat-chested, boyish-looking young women often made the most of their looks by adopting male attire. The figure in the center, wearing a formal black-and-white evening suit, is recognizable as a woman only by her elegant feminine shoes. This may have been a subconscious attempt to redress the postwar imbalance of men and women.

Independent women, especially among the literary set, adopted men's jackets, vests, ties, and monocles, worn with skirts. This included the Paris-based lesbian writer Radclyffe Hall and various artists. Like the Bloomer costume of the 1890s, the fashion was caricatured mercilessly.

Men's Dress Reform

By the end of the twenties, it was clear that although women's dress reform had revolutionized female roles in society, menswear lagged far behind. Various reform groups were set up to rectify this, including the Men's Dress Reform Party. Although this received much publicity and heated debates followed its formation in 1929, its impact was mainly among theorists, and its ideas were never widely adopted. The real advances in men's alternative dress in the 1920s came from the fashions worn by men in positions of influence and those in the public eye, such as sportsmen, actors, and writers.

We have already seen how the Prince of Wales influenced fashion on both sides of the Atlantic by, for example, his stylish adoption of the Fair Isle sweater and how the leather jackets of aviators, heroes of the modern age, filtered into more casual civilian wear. Tennis, too, had a huge following in the 1920s and a corresponding effect on fashion. In 1926, French International champion René Lacoste pioneered the soft-collared and short-sleeved tennis (or polo) shirt still worn today, with the same alligator motif (derived from Lacoste's nickname, the "Crocodile"). US tennis champion Bill Tilden popularized the tennis sweater—a cream or white cable-knit sweater with bands of color at collar and waist.

▲Athletic René Lacoste was a sports star in his own right, as well as the originator of the famous alligator logo.

◀Clean-cut, athletic Bill Tilden, twice winner of Wimbledon along with ten other major tournaments, wearing the V-necked sweater he helped to popularize.

▲These men's traveling clothes, in loud checks and stripes and rich, strong, vibrant colors, would have been considered extremely eccentric for ordinary wear. The anonymity of traveling, however, made them acceptable.

Noel Coward with Gertrude Lawrence in his play *Private Lives.* Trading on the traditional image of theater people as bohemian, Coward set the tone for a softer male image, especially in his trademark silk dressing gowns.

The Prince of Wales wore one for informal occasions, thus encouraging its adoption for casual wear as well as sportswear.

Many of these less restrictive garments have remained elements of stylish dressing ever since the 1920s, a decade when innovations in fashion stemmed from the occupations, sports, and pastimes of the upper classes. The age of fashion movements coming from the street and work wear did not arrive until much later in the century.

In Conclusion

Fashion was made available to a broader sector of the public as a result of modern retail policies and the idea that consumerism meant emancipation. Lighter garments of simpler cut and the electrification of the factories also made mass production possible. In many ways, the twenties established the themes and marketing policies that would be developed in the post-World War II period and that are so familiar to us today.

◄ In simple, peasant-inspired dress, our hostess is probably holding a salon in her perfect "alternative" interior. She has painted furniture and a needlepoint armchair in a riot of color, and even the teapot and dishes are of the latest rounded design.

Chronology

News

1920 Prohibition begins in USA.
League of Nations has its first session.

1921 Lenin introduces new economic policy in Russia.
Partition of Ireland.
First birth control clinic in London founded by Marie Stopes.

1922 America's first female senator.
Mussolini becomes the first Fascist dictator in Europe.
Mahatma Ghandi imprisoned for taking an anti-British stance.
USSR formed.

1923 Collapse of deutsch mark gives rise to protesting factions, including Nazis.
Ku Klux Klan reign of terror in America.
Progress in public health: tetanus and diphtheria immunization introduced.

1924 Passenger air travel begins.
British Empire Exhibition held at Wembley.
Olympic Games, Paris.

1925 Hitler's *Mein Kampf* published.
Britain returns to the Gold Standard.
Cocktails from America are taken up by smart society in Western Europe.
New homes are being installed with electricity.

1926 General Strike in Britain.
Death of Rudolph Valentino.
Modernization/Westernization in Turkey.
Scotsman John Logie Baird demonstrates the first successful television system to scientists in London.

1927 American Charles Lindbergh makes first solo flight across the Atlantic.
Freestyle, barefoot dancer Isadora Duncan is killed.
Kuomintang takes Shanghai, afterward Red Army is set up in China.

1928 "Flapper vote" is made law in Britain.
Indian National Congress demands Dominion status for India.
Stalin launches Five Year Plan; Trotsky is exiled.
Herbert Hoover becomes U.S. President.

1929 Wall Street Crash.
St. Valentine's Day Massacre, Chicago.
Second Labour Government in Britain; first woman cabinet minister appointed.
Arab-Jewish rioting in Palestine.
Graf Zeppelin makes around-the-world flight.

Events

First radio broadcasts.
French tennis star Suzanne Lenglen wins Wimbledon for second year running.
Charlie Chaplin's first full-length film, *The Kid*.

Expansion of public sports grounds, golf courses, etc.
Albert Einstein awarded Nobel Prize for physics; his Theory of Relativity is published.

Fleet Street newspaper "circulation war" in London.
American Johnny Weissmuller (the original Tarzan) is first man to swim 100 meters in under a minute.
Egyptian boy-king Tutankhamen's tomb discovered.

First full-scale exhibition of Bauhaus work; Schlemmer's *Mechanical Ballet* is performed.

Noel Coward's play *The Vortex* is staged in London.
George Gershwin composes "Rhapsody in Blue": orchestrated jazz.
Paris fashion and arts meet in Diaghilev's *Le Train Bleu* ballet: stage curtain by Picasso, sportswear by Coco Chanel.
Michael Arlen's *The Green Hat* is published.

Art Deco exhibition held in Paris.
Charleston and Black Bottom arrive in Europe, taking over from the waltz and fox trot.
Louis Armstrong forms the Hot Fives jazz band.
F. Scott Fitzgerald's *The Great Gatsby* is published.

Fritz Lang's film *Metropolis* is released.
Margaret Kennedy's novel *The Constant Nymph* is published.
A. A. Milne writes *Winnie the Pooh.*

Warner Brothers make the first "talkie," *The Jazz Singer*, starring Al Jolson.
Henry Seagrave exceeds 200 mph in land speed bid.

D. H. Lawrence's *Lady Chatterley's Lover* banned in Britain.
Mickey Mouse created, to join Felix the Cat in Walt Disney's menagerie.

Salvador Dali makes his first surrealist film, *Un Chien Andalou*.
Kodak produces first 16 mm color photographic film (but popular box cameras still restricted to black and white) .

Fashion

Chanel's pioneering jersey sweater and pleated skirt.
Ensembles are now accepted as easy wear.
Debutante Daisy Fellows challenges convention wearing black when presented to the Queen at Buckingham Palace instead of the traditional white.

Dress Essentials magazine features scarves among accessories; color coordination becomes a conscious feature of the average woman's wardrobe.

The Prince of Wales now orders all his trousers to be made with cuffs, and (unlike his father) wears suits in town.
East European folk embroideries inspire the peasant look in women's wear.

Soviet Atelier of Fashion is formed.
Bobbed hair becomes the rage.
Tutmania takes off with "Tutankhamen" overblouses, Egyptian colors, scarab and lotus jewelry, etc.

The Textile Color Card Association of the United States is formed, an attempt to establish a standard system of colors identified by numbers.

Vogue's first feature on the "little black dress".
"Oxford bags" are worn by young graduates.
The hemline is the shortest in history.
US production of rayon viscose reaches 53 million pounds for the year.

More masculine elements enter female dress.
The severely short "Eton crop" haircut ousts bobbed hair.
Jeanne Lanvin opens first boutique for men.

Patent leather shoes are new.
Nancy Cunard, wearing African bangles to the elbows, is photographed by Man Ray.

The press declares "fever chart" hemlines.
Hat brims return to fashion.
The first of Schiaparelli's *trompe l'oeil* sweaters are a resounding success.

Men's Dress Reform Party is founded in Britain.
A new femininity: hemlines are now longer for daywear, as well as evening.

Glossary

Art Deco A geometric style of decorative art. The term was coined from the *Exposition des Arts Décoratifs et Industriels Modernes,* Paris, 1925.

Avant-garde (French for vanguard) Supporting or expressing the newest ideas and techniques in an art.

Batik A textile onto which the design is drawn in wax before dyeing.

Bauhaus German school of art and architecture, founded by Walter Gropius in 1919, forced to close under the Nazis in 1933.

Bianchini-Férier Lyons textile firm. Through 1920s produced printed and woven fashion fabrics including designs by French painter Raoul Dufy.

Callot Soeurs Three sisters of Russian ancestry who in 1890s set up Paris fashion house. Exotic evening dresses combining Chinese motifs, lavish embroidery, plumes, lace and antique textiles.

Carnegie, Hattie (1889–1956) American designer who assembled her first fashion collection in 1919—neat gray worsted suits, straight skirts, jeweled buttons were her hallmark. In 1928 she launched ready-to-wear collections.

Chanel, Gabrielle ("Coco") (1873–1971) French designer, established in the Paris couture business by 1919. Known for simple, functional garments of wool jersey, especially sweaters and pleated skirts. Recognized the importance of sportswear, put the little black dress on the map, and encouraged the fashion for costume jewelry.

Constructivism Dynamic, very exact, non-representational style of art bridging art and industry that originated in Russia.

Cubism Movement in painting seeking to represent several aspects of the same object (or group of objects) viewed from different angles within one composition, using cubes and other solid geometrical figures.

Delaunay, Sonia (1885–1979) Brought up in Russia, studied drawing in Germany and painting in Paris. She made her first "simultaneous" paintings in 1912 and in the 1920s she translated this abstract art into fabric and fashion designs.

Diaghilev, Serge (1872–1929) Russian, a member of the artistic and literary circle of St. Petersburg. Created the Ballets Russes, which first performed Paris in 1909. he worked with designer Leon Bakst, commissioned artists like Sonia Delaunay and Pablo Picasso to design sets and costumes for new ballets.

Erté (Romain de Tirtoff: 1892–1990) Russian-born fashion illustrator and designer of fantastic sets and costumes for the Folies Bergères revues in Paris, and later their American equivalent, the Ziegfeld Follies.

Ferragamo, Salvatore (1898–1960) Innovative Italian shoe designer and manufacturer, who made a name for himself in Hollywood, then set up company in Florence, Italy in 1927.

Fortuny, Mariano (1871–1949) Spanish, but working in Venice from 1907, painter and stage designer as well as creator of textiles and dress. Designed simple garments with rich fabric effects and details such as lace and eyelet fastenings weighted with Venetian glass beads.

Futurism Art movement claiming to anticipate or point the way to the future. Futurist artists created a feeling of dynamic motion in their works.

Haute Couture Most expensive sector of the fashion industry, in which clothes directly based on "model" garments are custom made.

Lanvin, Jeanne (1867–1946) French couturier, well known by 1915 for romantic "robe de style" inspired by dresses designed for young girls. Opened boutique for men's clothes in 1926. Responsible for installation of Pavillon d'Elegance at the 1925 Art Deco exhibition.

Lelong, Lucien French couturier. Opened fashion house 1923. Created models for his wife, the society beauty Princess Natalie Paley, who publicized his style.

Lepape, Georges (1887–1971) One of the leading French fashion illustrators.

Lucile (Lucy Wallace Duff Gordon) (c. 1870–1935) Canadian born, first London-based fashion designer of international repute. Claimed credit for liberating women from corsets and introducing new bright colors. Lucile also designed luxurious lingerie.

Molyneux, Edward (1891–1974) British, trained by Lucile. Set up his own establishment in Paris in 1919, creating classic clothes of restrained elegance.

Patou, Jean (1880–1936) French couturier involved in fashion design from 1914. Formed his own establishment in 1919. One of first Parisian couturiers to market wholesale copies of original models.

Poiret, Paul (1879–1943) Worked with Paris houses of Doucet and Worth before opening his own salon in 1904. Created clothes of simple cut, brilliant colors, and rich textures. The first couturier to introduce perfume.

Post-impressionism Art movement following impressionism, aiming to express the spiritual quality of things, rather than a realistic representation of their physical appearance.

Rodchenko, Alexander (1891–1956) Russian Constructivist involved in socially useful applications of art after the 1917 Revolution—especially graphics and photography.

Rodier French company founded by Paul Rodier, said to have produced 5,000 textile designs per year for innovative and exclusive haute couture fabrics, mostly in wool and linen. He employed cottage hand weavers in Picardy.

Schiaparelli, Elsa (1890–1972) Born in Rome, Schiaparelli developed reputation as fashion designer in Paris from c. 1928. She was in the vanguard of new fashionable silhouettes, eg, broad shoulders c. 1930; much work inspired by Salvador Dalí and the Surrealist movement.

Surrealism From c. 1919, a movement in French art and literature that sought to draw on the subconscious, escaping the control of reasoning or preconception.

Vionnet, Madeleine (1876–1939) French designer apprenticed in a fashion house at age 12. Worked for Doucet and Callot before opening her own house in 1912.

Worth The first great couture house, founded in Paris in 1858 by English-born Charles Frederick Worth (1826–1895), later run by his sons and grandsons. There were branches in all major capitals of Europe by 1900. Worth dressed royalty and created very dignified clothes.

Further Reading

Many books have been published on the 1920s and on fashions in the decade. Magazines and movies are also excellent sources of information.

Adult General Reference Sources

Blum, Stella. *Everyday Fashions of the Twenties* (Dover, 1981)

Calasibetta, Charlotte. *Essential Terms of Fashion: A Collection of Definitions* (Fairchild, 1985)

Calasibetta, *Charlotte. Fairchild's Dictionary of Fashion* (Fairchild, 2nd ed, 1988)

Cumming, Valerie. *Understanding Fashion History* (Chrysalis, 2004)

Ewing, Elizabeth. *History of Twentieth Century Fashion*, revised by Alice Mackrell (Batsford, 4th ed, 2001)

Gold, Annalee. *90 Years of Fashion* (Fairchild, 1990)

Laver, James. *Costume and Fashion* (Thames & Hudson, 1995)

O'Hara, Georgina. *The Encyclopedia of Fashion* (Harry N. Abrams, 1986)

Peacock, John. *Twentieth Century Fashion: The Complete Sourcebook* (Thames & Hudson, 1993)

Peacock, John. *Fashion Sourcebook: the 1920s* (Thames & Hudson, 1997)

Peacock, John. *Men's Fashion: The Complete sourcebook* (Emerald, 1997)

Peacock, John. *Fashion Accessories: The Complete 20th century sourcebook* (Thames & Hudson, 2000)

Stegemeyer, Anne. *Who's Who in Fashion*, (Fairchild, 4th ed, 2003)

Trahey, Jane (ed.) Harper's Bazaar: *100 Years of the American Female* (Random House, 1967)

Watson, Linda. *Twentieth-century Fashion* (Firefly, 2004)

Young Adult Sources

Blackman, Cally. *Twentieth Century Fashion: the 20s and 30s* (Heinemann Library, 1999)

Mee, Sue. *Twentieth Century Fashion: 1900-20* (Heinemann Library, 1999)

Ruby, Jennifer. *The 1920s and 1930s, Costume in Context series* (David & Charles, 1989)

Wilcox, R. Turner. *Five Centuries of American Costume* (Scribner's, 1963)

Acknowledgments

The Publishers would like to thank the following for permission to reproduce illustrations: Art Archive 6b, 8t, 12br, 24, 25, 59b; B.T. Batsford 26t, 29l, 30b, 32b, 34l, 40, 41tl, 41b, 42, 45l, 56l; Getty Images 28, 30t, 43tl, 49, 53l, 54b, 57t; Kobal Collection 35, 38, 39r; Lighthorne Pictures 10b, 13, 17, 18bl, 19, 23t, 31l, 33b, 41tr, 45r, 48t, 50t, 56tr, 57b, 58br; Mary Evans Picture Library 10t, 11t, 11b, 12t, 14, 15, 16, 20, 29r, 33tl, 44b, 46b, 47, 50b, 51, 55; Pictorial Press 12bl; Popperfoto 18t, 26b, 34r, 39l, 43b, 58t, 58bl, 59t; Topfoto 8b,11c, 18br, 23b, 32t, 52t; Victoria & Albert Museum 7t, 43tr, 54t; Vintage Magazine Co. 6t, 7b, 9, 21, 22, 27, 31r, 33tr, 37, 44t, 46t, 48b, 52b, 53r, 56br

Key: b=bottom, t=top, l=left, r=right

Index

Numbers in *italics* refer to illustrations.

African influence 23, 44, 45, 48
Arden, Elizabeth 48
Armstrong, Louis 25
Art Deco 12, *12*, 20, 46, *47*
Ascot 11
Astaire, Fred 35, *35*

Baker, Josephine 22, 23, 24, 25, *43*
Banky, Vilma *37*
Banton, Travis 39
Bara, Theda 36
Barnes, Djuna 56
batik 23, 45
Beaton, Cecil 24, 54
Beer, House of *13*
Bianchini-Férier 45
Black Bottom 19, *19*, 44
bohemian style 30, *31*, 56, *56*, 57, 59
Bow, Clara 36, *39*
Brooks, Louise 36, *39*
Brooks Brothers 32
Burberry 8, *8*

Callot Soeurs 40, 46
Calloway, Cab 25
Capone, Al 8, 24, 32, *32*
Carnegie, Hattie 43
Chanel, Gabrielle (Coco) 11–12, *12*, 19, 24, 39, 40, 41, 50, 52
Charleston *7*, 44
cloche hats 8, *30*
Communism 10
Constructivism 20, 29
consumerism 7, 16–17, *18*
Corbusier, Le 19, 20
cosmetics 48
Cotton Club 25, *25*
Coward, Noel 57, 59, *59*
cross-dressing 57, *57*
Cubism 23
Cunard, Nancy 8

Dalí, Salvador 24, 41
Delaunay, Sonia 29
Diaghilev, Serge 23, 24, 46
Dolly Sisters *26*

Doucet, Jacques 24, 40
Dufy, Raoul *18*, 45, 54
Duncan, Raymond 57

East European style 45, *56*
Egyptian style 26, *27*, 44, *44*, *46*
Ellington, Duke 25
Erté *24*
Eton crop 30
evening wear 12, 14, 31, 35, 41, 42, 45, 59
"Everybody's Doing It Now" 5

Fascism 10
Fair Isle 32, *32*, 41, 50, 58
fashion industry 11, 12–15, 22, 40–43
fashion photography 24
Ferragamo, Salvatore 22, 39
Fitzgerald, F. Scott 31, 32
Flappers 6, 28, 30, 44
Folies Bergères 24
Ford, Henry 6, 19
Fortuny, Mariano 46
Futurism 23

Gandhi, Mohandas K. 10
gangsters 8
Garbo, Greta 36, *38*
Germany 8
Gershwin, George 26, 36
Gish, Lillian 36
Grant, Duncan 56
Great Gatsby, The 32, *33*
Greenwich Village 56
Greer, Howard 39

Harlem 22, 25
Hartnell, Norman *45*
haute couture 13–15
Heim, Jacques 29
Hollywood 11, 19, 39

"It Girl" 36
Italy 10, 22

jazz 6, 7, 22, 25, 44
Jazz Singer, The 25
Jolson, Al 25

Kemal, Mustafa (Atatürk) 10
knickers 32, 57
Ku Klux Klan 10

Lacoste, René 58, *58*
Lanvin, Jeanne 12, 38, 41, 43
Lawrence, Gertrude 36
Lee, Kitty *30*
Lelong, Lucien 31, 43
Lenglen, Suzanne 52
Lepape, Georges 24
London 11, 22, 24, 26, 49, 50, 56
Lucile (Lady Duff Gordon) 40

machine age 19–20, 22
mass production 6–7, 15–16, 19, 20
Melba, Dame Nellie 7
Men's Dress Reform Party 58
Miller, Lee 24
Mills, Lady Dorothy 56
Mistinguette 17
Modernism 19
Molyneux, Edward 31, 38
Monaco, Ugo Io 15
motoring 6, *6*, 8, *8*, 31
movies 36, 39
Mussolini, Benito 10

Nazis 8
Negri, Pola 36, 42
New York 25, 26, 32, 42

Olympic Games 20
Original Dixieland Jazz Band 22, 26
Oxford bags 29, *29*

Palm Beach 11, 53
Paris 11, 12, 13, *13*, 17, 22, 23, 24, 31, 43
Paris Exhibition (1925) 12
Patou, Jean 13, 15, 52
Piatti, Carlo 15
Picasso, Pablo 23
Poiret, Paul 13, 40, *40*, *41*, 43, 46
Pound, Ezra 30
Prince of Wales 32, 35, 58, 59

Printemps, Yvonne 38
Prohibition 7, 8, 24

radio 7
Ray, Man 24
Régny, Jane 53
Revue Nègre 22
Rodchenko, Alexander 10
Rubinstein, Helena 48

Saleeby, Dr. 50, 52
Sanger, Margaret 11
Savile Row 32, 36
Schiaparelli, Elsa 24, 40–41, 42, 43
sewing machines 17, *17*
Sickert, Walter 56
sportswear *6*, 8, *21*, 32, 50, *50*, 51, 52, *52*, 53, *53*, 54, 55, *55*, *58*, 59
Steichen, Edward 22, 24
Stepanova, Varvara 20, 29, 54
Stopes, Dr. Marie 11
St. Valentine's Day Massacre 24
Surrealism 23, 24, 41
Swanson, Gloria, 11, 36
synthetic fabrics 48

Tarzan 20, 36
Tilden, Bill 58
Tutankhamen 44
"Tutmania" 44, 46

USSR 10, *10*, 16, 20

Valentino, Rudolph *34*, 36
Vienna 29
Vionnet, Madeleine 15, 22, *23*, 40, 42, *42*

Walker, Madame C. J. 48
Wall Street Crash 13, 26, *26*, 48
Weissmuller, Johnny 20, 36
Whiteman, Paul 26
Wiener Werkstätte 29
World War I 6, 11, 30, 48, 57
influence on fashion 7–8, 40, 48
Worth, Charles 14, 20, 40, 53

Ziegfeld Follies 24